This book belongs to

....

The Duckling and Other Stories

How this collection works

This *Biff, Chip and Kipper* collection is one of a series of four books at **Read with Oxford Stage 2**. It is divided into two distinct halves.

The first half focuses on phonics, with two stories written in line with the phonics your child will have learned at school: *The Duckling* and *Quick! Quick!* The second half contains two stories that use everyday language: *The Monster Hunt* and *The Old Tree Stump*. These stories help to broaden your child's wider reading experience. There are also fun activities to enjoy throughout the book.

How to use this book

Find a time to read with your child when they are not too tired and are happy to concentrate for about ten to fifteen minutes. Reading at this stage should be a shared and enjoyable experience. It is best to choose just one story for each session.

There are tips for each part of the book to help you make the most of the stories and activities. The tips for reading on pages 6 and 28 show you how to introduce your child to the phonics stories.

The tips for reading on pages 50 and 72 explain how you can best approach reading the stories that use a wider vocabulary. At the end of each of the four stories you will find four 'Talk about the story' questions. These will help your child to think about what they have read, and to relate the story to their own experiences. The questions are followed by a fun activity.

Enjoy sharing the stories!

Authors and illustrators

The Duckling written by Roderick Hunt, illustrated by Nick Schon
Quick, Quick! written by Roderick Hunt, illustrated by Nick Schon
The Monster Hunt written by Cynthia Rider, illustrated by Alex Brychta
The Old Tree Stump written by Roderick Hunt, illustrated by Alex Brychta

OXFORD
UNIVERSITY PRESS

Great Clarendon Street, Oxford, OX2 6DP, United Kingdom

Oxford University Press is a department of the University
of Oxford. It furthers the University's objective of excellence
in research, scholarship, and education by publishing
worldwide. Oxford is a registered trade mark of Oxford
University Press in the UK and in certain other countries

The Old Tree Stump, *Quick, Quick!*, *The Duckling* text © Roderick Hunt
2005, 2007, 2014
The Monster Hunt text © Cynthia Rider 2006

The Old Tree Stump, *The Monster Hunt*, illustrations © Alex Brychta 2005, 2006
Quick, Quick! illustrations © Alex Brychta and Nick Schon 2007
The Duckling illustrations by Nick Schon © Oxford University Press 2014

The Old Tree Stump first published in 2005
The Monster Hunt first published in 2006
Quick, Quick! first published in 2007
The Duckling first published in 2014

This Edition first published in 2018

British Library Cataloguing in Publication Data
Data available

ISBN: 978-0-19-276422-5

10 9 8 7 6 5 4 3 2 1

Paper used in the production of this book is a natural, recyclable product
made from wood grown in sustainable forests. The manufacturing process
conforms to the environmental regulations of the country of origin.

Printed in China

Acknowledgements

Series Editors: Annemarie Young and Kate Ruttle

Contents

OXFORD
UNIVERSITY PRESS

Phonics

Children learn best when reading is relaxed and enjoyable.

- Talk about the title and the picture on page 7, and read the speech bubble at the bottom of that page.

- Identify the letter pattern *ing* in the title and talk about the sound it makes when you read it.

- Look at the *sh*, *ch*, *qu* and *ing* words on page 8. Say the sounds in each word and then say the word (e.g. *qu-a-ck*, *quack*).

- Read the story and find the words with the letters *sh*, *ch*, *qu* and *ing* in them.

- Talk about the story and do the fun activity on page 26.

Children enjoy re-reading stories and this helps to build their confidence.

Have fun!

After you have read the story, find the frog in every picture.

The main sounds practised in this story are 'sh' as in *shock* and rubbish, 'ch ' as in *check*, 'qu' as in *quack* and 'ing' as in *duckling*.

For more activities, free eBooks and practical advice to help your child progress with reading visit **oxfordowl.co.uk**

6

The Duckling

What happened to the duckling?

Say the sounds and read these words.

shock   rubbi**sh**

quack   duckl**ing**

quick   **ch**eck

8

Wilma had a shock.

The pond was a mess.

Dad put the rubbish in the bin.

Wilma fed the ducks.

But a duckling was missing.

The duckling was stuck.

It had its leg in a bag.

The bag was filling up.

The duckling was sinking.

Wilma was upset.

Dad got the net.

Dad went into the pond.

Dad put the duckling into
the net.

They got the bag off
the duckling.

Dad was wet!

They put the duckling
back into the pond.

Talk about the story

What was wrong with the duckling?

Why was Wilma upset?

What did Dad do?

What creatures have you helped?

Spot the difference

Find the five differences in the pictures of Dad.

Tips for reading *Quick! Quick!*

Children learn best when reading is relaxed and enjoyable.

- Talk about the title and the picture on page 29, and read the speech bubble.

- Identify the letter pattern *qu* in the title and talk about the sound it makes when you read it.

- Look at the *qu*, *ou* and *ck* words on page 30. Say the sounds in each word and then say the word (e.g. *qu-i-ck*, *quick*; *ou-t*, *out*).

- Read the story together, then find the words with *qu*, *ou* and *ck*.

- Talk about the story and do the maze on page 48.

Children enjoy re-reading stories and this helps to build their confidence.

Have fun!

After you have read the story, find the ants in five of the pictures.

The main sounds practised in this story are 'qu' as in *quick*, and 'ou' as in *out*. The other sound practised is 'ck' as in *quick*.

 For more activities, free eBooks and practical advice to help your child progress with reading visit **oxfordowl.co.uk**

Quick! Quick!

Quick! Kipper
is stuck!

Say the sounds and read these words.

quick   out

ouch   stuck

stick   jack

The ball shot off.

"I can get it," said Kipper.

But Kipper got stuck.

Quick, get me out.

Biff ran to get Dad.

Quick, quick.

"Kipper is stuck," said Biff.

"I can get him out," said Dad.

"He is still stuck," said Biff.

Dad rang Mum.

"Kipper is stuck," said Dad.

Mum got a big stick.

"Ouch," said Kipper. "I am still stuck."

Wilma ran to get her dad.

"Kipper is stuck," said Wilma.

Wilma's dad got his jack.

Kipper got out.

Dad was stuck.

Talk about the story

How did Kipper get stuck?

What did Wilma's dad use to get Kipper out?

Why did Dad get stuck?

Have you got stuck before? Where?

A maze

Help Kipper get the ball.

Stories for Wider Reading

Tips for reading the stories together

These two stories use simple everyday language. You can help your child to read any more challenging words in the context of the story. Children enjoy re-reading stories and this helps to build their confidence and their vocabulary.

Tips for reading *The Monster Hunt*

- Talk about the title and the speech bubble on page 51, and look through the pictures so that your child can see what the story is about.
- Read the story together, encouraging your child to read as much as they can with you.
- Give lots of praise as your child reads with you, and help them when necessary.
- If your child gets stuck on a word that is easily decodable, encourage them to say the sounds and then blend them together to read the word. Read the whole sentence again. Focus on the meaning. If the word is not decodable, or is still too tricky, just read the word for them and move on.
- When you've finished reading the story, talk about it with your child, using the 'Talk about the story' questions at the end.
- Do the activity on page 70.
- Re-read the story later, again encouraging your child to read as much of it as they can.

After you have read
The Monster Hunt, find
the mouse in every picture.

Have fun!

This story includes these useful
common words:

children   come   saw   went

For more activities, free eBooks
and practical advice to help
your child progress with reading
visit **oxfordowl.co.uk**

The Monster Hunt

Can the children get the monster?

Gran took the children on
a monster hunt.

Biff saw some monster
footprints.

Chip saw a monster glove, and...

... Kipper saw the monster!

"Come on," said Gran.
"Let's get that monster!"

The monster ran.
It ran up the hill.

It ran into the mill…
and hid.

"Come on," said Chip.
"Let's get that monster!"

They went into the mill.

"Ssh!" said Gran.

"I can see the monster's tail."

Gran pulled the monster's tail.
"Got you!" she said.

"AARGH!" said the monster.

Crash! went a sack.
Crash! went the monster.

The monster looked at the
children. "Help!" he said.

"Monsters!"

Talk about the story

Why do you think Gran and the children went on a monster hunt?

How did the children know which way the monster had gone?

How would you feel if you got covered in flour?

Would you like to go on a monster hunt? What would you do if you caught the monster?

Picture puzzle

Match the monster to its shadow.

Tips for reading *The Old Tree Stump*

- Talk about the title and the speech bubble on page 73, and look through the pictures so that your child can see what the story is about.

- Read the story together, encouraging your child to read as much as they can with you.

- Give lots of praise as your child reads with you, and help them when necessary.

- If your child gets stuck on a word that is easily decodable, encourage them to say the sounds and then blend them together to read the word. Read the whole sentence again. Focus on the meaning. If the word is not decodable, or is still too tricky, just read the word for them and move on.

- Read the whole sentence again. Focus on the meaning.

- When you've finished reading the story, talk about it with your child, using the 'Talk about the story' questions at the end.

- Do the activity on pages 92.

Have fun!

- Re-read the story later, again encouraging your child to read as much of it as they can.

After you have read the story, find these ten minibeasts in the pictures.

This story includes these useful common words:

come   didn't   pull   want

For more activities, free eBooks and practical advice to help your child progress with reading visit **oxfordowl.co.uk**

The Old Tree Stump

The old tree stump has to go!

"That old stump has to go,"
said Dad.

Dad pulled the old stump,
but it didn't come up.

Dad called Mum to help.
"I'll push it. You pull it,"
said Dad.

"When I say pull," said Dad,
"I want you to pull!"

Mum pulled and pulled, but
the stump didn't come up.

Dad called Biff.

"I want you to pull," said Dad.

Mum and Biff pulled...
but the stump *still* didn't
come up.

Dad wanted Chip to help.
"When I shout pull," said Dad,
"I want you to pull."

They all pulled...
but the stump *still* didn't
come up.

Kipper wanted to help.
"Come on, then," said Dad.
"When I shout pull... PULL!"

They pulled and they pulled...
but the stump *still* didn't
come up.

"I'll pull as well," said Dad.
"When I yell pull... PULL!"

They all pulled and pulled...
but the stump *still* didn't
come up.

Floppy saw a bone.
He dug and he dug, and...

... up came the stump!

BUMP!

"Good old Floppy!" said Chip.

Talk about the story

How did the stump come up in the end?

Which part of the story did you find the funniest?

Have you ever read the Enormous Turnip? How is it like this story?

What jobs do you help with at home?

Picture puzzle

Which things don't rhyme with snail?

Remembering the stories together

Encourage your child to remember and retell the stories in this book. You could ask questions like these:

- Who are the characters in the story?
- What happens at the beginning of the story?

- What happens next?
- How does the story end?
- What was your favourite part of the story? Why?

Story prompts

When talking to your child about the stories, you could use these more detailed reminders to help them remember the exact sequence of events. Turn the statements below into questions, so that your child can give you the answers. For example, *What is the pond covered with? What does Wilma do while Dad tidies up?* And so on …

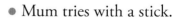

The Duckling

- The pond is covered in rubbish.
- Dad tidies up while Wilma feeds the ducks.
- She notices that one of the ducklings is missing!

- She realises that the duckling is stuck in a plastic bag and is sinking.
- Dad goes into the pond and gets the bag off the duckling.
- They put the duckling back into the pond.

Quick, Quick!

- The children are playing football, but the ball goes over the fence.
- Kipper thinks he can get the ball, but he gets stuck.
- Dad tries to get him out, but he can't do it.

- Mum tries with a stick.
- Wilma goes to get her dad and he manages to get Kipper out.
- Then Dad gets stuck!

The Monster Hunt

- Gran takes the children on a monster hunt.
- Kipper sees the monster and they chase after him.
- The monster runs into the mill to hide.
- Gran pulls the monster's tail and the monster falls and gets covered in flour!

- They all get covered in flour and now they all look like monsters!

The Old Tree Stump

- Dad tries to pull up a tree stump with a rope.
- Mum helps him pull, but nothing happens.
- The children pull as well, but still nothing happens.

- Floppy sees a bone under the stump and digs and digs.
- Suddenly the stump comes out and they all fall over!

You could now encourage your child to create a 'story map' of each story, drawing and colouring all the key parts of them. This will help them to identify the main elements of the stories and learn to create their own stories.